Using Windows
Media Player 11

Other Titles of Interest from Bernard Babani (publishing) Ltd

Using Windows
Media Player 11

by

Tony Campbell

Bernard Babani (publishing) Ltd

The Grampians

Shepherds Bush Road

London W6 7NF

England

www.babanibooks.com

Please Note

Although every care has been taken with the production of this book to ensure that any projects, designs, modifications and/or programs, etc., contained herewith, operate in a correct and safe manner and also that any components specified are normally available in Great Britain, the Publishers and Author(s) do not accept responsibility in any way for the failure (including fault in design) of any project, design, modification or program to work correctly or to cause damage to any equipment that it may be connected to or used in conjunction with, or in respect of any other damage or injury that may be so caused, nor do the Publishers accept responsibility in any way for the failure to obtain specified components.

Notice is also given that if equipment that is still under warranty is modified in any way or used or connected with home-built equipment then that warranty may be void.

First Published – December 2006

ISBN: 978 0 85934 573 6

British Library Cataloguing in Publication Data:

A catalogue record for this book is available from the British Library

Cover Design by George Arthur

Printed and Bound in Great Britain by CPD

About this Book

Media Player 11 is the latest, and by far the best, iteration of Microsoft's free multimedia player. The greatly improved interface substantially enhances its previously very good library functionality, facilitating better grouping and sorting of your media files. Enhanced functionality in terms of networking and device synchronisation take MP3 and video management to a new level, including the dynamic export of subsets of media to portable devices through automatically generated playlists.

Media Player 11 is a timely response to Apple's proprietary iPod + iTunes solution for digital video and audio content management and this book explains just how Media Player works in conjunction with its associated technologies.

At the time of writing, Microsoft's Media Player 11 was available as a free download for Windows XP users and is to be included with all versions of Microsoft Vista.

Conventions

Throughout this book, you will see a number of information boxes, bounded with either a double line like this...

DESIGNATING A WARNING

...or indeed, a single line, like this...

DESIGNATING A NOTE, POINT OF INTEREST OR USEFUL TIP

Procedures and walkthroughs are shown as numerical lists, like this:

1. Step 1
2. Step 2

All diagrams and figures have a two-digit reference number containing the chapter number, followed by the figure number within that chapter. For example, Figure 1-1 represents the first figure in Chapter 1.

About the Author

Tony Campbell has been in IT for a very long time, consulting for large and small companies alike over the past few decades. He is the author of a variety of IT books (including the bestselling *Windows Vista: Beyond the Manual*; http://www.vista.beyondthemanual.com) and magazine articles, and he also specialises in designing large-scale, highly secure solutions for his customers, based mainly upon (but not limited to) Microsoft client/server technologies.

Over the course of his career, he has worked in many parts of the IT industry and gained considerable experience in both the practical and written side of the job.

Today, Tony mainly writes for his living, although he still enjoys real-world customer contact when engagements present themselves.

Visit Tony's Windows Vista blog site and contact him there if you want to discuss any aspect of his work:

http://www.vista.beyondthemanual.com

Tony lives in Hampshire with his wife, Sharon and daughter Lara.

Acknowledgements

Thanks again to everyone who helped me with the production of this book.

Especially, I'd like to thank my wife, Sharon for her support, and special thanks for helping me get this printed and off to the publisher before the Christmas holidays.

In addition, special thanks go to Lara for being such an angel and helping me test Media Player with some of her music.

For Lara, the pop star.

Trademarks

Microsoft, Windows XP, Windows Vista, Windows Media Player and **Zune** are either registered trademarks or trademarks of the Microsoft Corporation.

All other brand and product names used in this book are recognised as trademarks, or registered trademarks of their respective companies.

Contents

1

Introducing Windows Media Player 11

The Windows Media Player has formed a fundamental part of Microsoft's digital media arsenal for many, many years, cited by consumers as one of the best media libraries and players on the market.

The latest version of Media Player (version 11), shipping as a core component of all versions of the Vista operating system and as a downloadable update to previous versions of the Windows operating system, delivers a total product facelift.

With a whole range of new capabilities supporting the latest video and audio formats (such as High Definition TV — HDTV) as well as having a much improved interface and a whole set of new metadata search and organisational features.

Figure 1-1 The new look of Media Player 11

The new interface is very much designed using the new look for Vista, meaning you get, even on Windows XP, a look at how the next generation of Microsoft operating systems and applications will appear to the user. Take a look at Figure 1-1 to see what this interface is like.

Downloading and Installing

You can download Media Player 11 from Microsoft's website from the following address:

http://www.microsoft.com/downloads

Make sure your system meets the minimum requirements for Media Player 11, shown here in Table 1-1.

Component	Minimum Required	Recommended
Operating System	Windows XP with Service Pack 2	Windows Vista
Processor Speed	233 MHz	1.5 GHz
RAM	64 MB	512 MB or more
Hard Disc Space	200 MB	60 GB
Optical Drive	CD or DVD	DVD ± RW
Modem	28.8 Kbps	Broadband
Sound Card	16-bit	24-bit surround
Monitor	SVGA (800 x 600)	SVGA or higher
Video Card	64 MB RAM and DirectX 9.0b	256 MB RAM and DirectX 9.0b or higher
Browser	IE 6.0 or Netscape 7.1	IE 6.0 or Netscape 7.1

Table 1-1 System requirements for installing Media Player 11

Installing Media Player

After you have downloaded Media Player 11 from the website, double-click on the installation file and follow the simple instructions for installing it on your PC. Progress is tracked throughout the installation, communicated back to you through an interactive interface that informs you of what's happening and how long it's going to take to complete, see Figure 1-2.

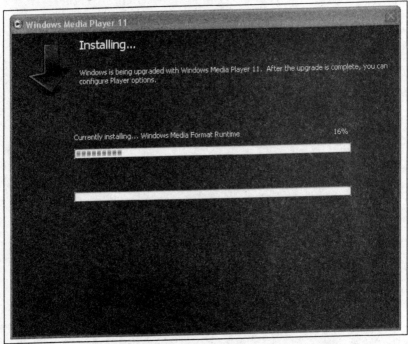

Figure 1-2 Track installation progress using
this simple interface

When the software has fully installed, the following phase is the initial setup, where you will configure fundamental settings, such as security and privacy preferences.

Running Media Player the First Time

Whether you are using Media Player on a Windows XP or Windows Vista system, the first time you start it you will need to run through a short setup routine to configure how the player looks, what the player is responsible for playing, and how it handles the all-important issue of security and privacy.

To start Media Player, do the following:

1. Click on the Start menu
2. Click on All Programs
3. Select Windows Media Player.

The first screen that you'll see when you run Media Player for the first time offers two options, (see Figure 1-3):

- *Express* setup
- *Custom* setup

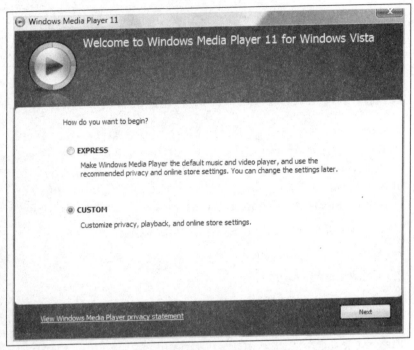

Figure 1-3 Select Express or Custom setup

For completeness, we will follow through the *Custom* setup routine as a way of introducing all the topics you need to be familiar with for understanding fully how Media Player works.

To start the setup, it's a simple matter of selecting the *Custom* radio button then clicking on the Next button.

The following screen, shown in Figure 1-4, entitled *Select Privacy Options*, has a variety of categories of settings you need to carefully consider before proceeding.

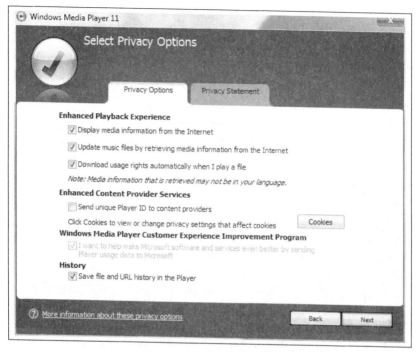

Figure 1-4 Privacy options allow you to configure what information you are willing to share with other users and online content stores

Privacy

The term *Privacy* refers to your ability to keep control over personal information about you, your family or your computer system and stop it becoming, as the antonym would suggest, public.

Information such as your bank account details or credit card numbers are obvious candidates for data you'd want to protect, however, there are many more information snippets pertaining to your private life that must remain under your direct control.

Take for example, the consequences of your email address getting into the wrong hands; if *they* don't know you exist, it's harder for *them* to target you. You might have previously considered you email address to be public information since you send it all over the world on the Internet each and every day. Nevertheless, spammers who are more than willing to part with money to get hold of 'live' email addresses will be waiting to pounce on this information from an email collection source. The next think you know, you inbox is filling up with adverts for unwanted products. If you do not let your email address become public, you won't get the same volume of spam. Sounds simple, doesn't it? You should realise, however, that many websites capture your email address as part of their registration process and can, without your knowledge, sell it on to third party companies.

For this very reason, applications that interact with third party companies or individuals on the Internet should be able to offer you, the user, the ability to select which information you want to keep private, and as importantly, which information you think can be seen as publicly available for use by whomever.

Throughout the rest of this book, you will see further references to maintaining privacy in Media Player. With the latest features in downloading content, online shopping and Digital Rights Management, privacy has certainly become one of today's "hot topics".

The following section explains the privacy settings that you need to consider before you start using Media Player in anger.

Here, I cover the default privacy settings for each item, as well as highlighting the highest security settings in each case.

Display Media Information from the Internet

This setting allows Media Player to request information on digital content from an online store. For this to work, Media Player sends the store an id *tag* from the CD or DVD you are using. The problem with this is that this might allow the music store to determine which CDs and DVDs you have in your collection. Take note, this setting does not only display information as the name suggests, it also interfaces with online services

The default setting for this information is *Permit* although selecting *Deny* is certainly the most secure.

Update Music Files by Retrieving Media Information from the Internet

Media Player automatically searches for missing content metadata on the Internet, such as album covers or track listings. If it locates the information, it is downloaded into your library.

This setting works in conjunction with the previous setting, *Display media information from the Internet*. If you configure the previous setting as *Deny*, you should also deny this one.

The default for this setting is *Permit*, although *Deny* is the more secure option.

Download Usage Rights Automatically when I Play or Sync a File

Media Usage Rights determine how you use the content you have purchased online.

If you *Permit* this, Media Player will automatically download the appropriate digital rights for the content, and playback of that content will be seamless. If you choose to *Deny* this freedom, you must obtain the necessary licence another way, either by email or CD or some other means.

It is not advisable that you deny this functionality unless you have a very good reason. In this case, the default setting is set to *Permit*, and I would recommend that the more secure setting profile should also be *Permit*, although *Deny* is most definitely the most secure.

Automatically Update Subscription Rights Before They Expire

If you have already obtained content that requires a digital licence, and that digital licence has an expiry date where the licence is renewable after the expiry date, Media Player will automatically detect this and request an updated licence from the issue authority.

Denying this will mean licensed content expires and is no longer available for playback.

The default setting for this is Permit, and it is advisable, from a usability perspective, you leave the setting as Permit even in high security environments.

Set Device Clock So That Subscription Files Can Sync

Media Player is capable of synchronising the internal digital clock on portable media devices, such as MP3 players or portable Media Center systems.

It is vitally important if you have a portfolio of licensed content where that content licence expires that system time on portable devices is managed correctly.

If you have such content you want to synchronise with a portable device, the default is *Permit*. If you do not want your PC reaching out and touching your portable devices and you would rather manage the time settings of the portable device yourself, select *Deny*.

Send Unique Player ID to Content Providers

This setting should be used to allow Media Player to send a unique ID to content stores whereby allowing those stores to recognise your system and adjust their service accordingly.

Many see this as a privacy violation; hence, the default setting is *Deny*. Nevertheless, some content providers might require this to be allowed to use their service; if this is the case, you will have to weigh up whether or not you believe this to be a breach of your privacy and whether you want this set to *Permit*.

The most secure setting in this case is certainly *Deny*.

I Want to Help Make Microsoft Software Services Even Better by Sending Player Usage Data to Microsoft

To take part in Microsoft's Customer Experience Improvement Program, you should *Permit* this setting. This anonymously notifies Microsoft as to how you are using Media Player with a guarantee from Microsoft that *no personal information* will ever be transmitted over the network.

Again, like most privacy settings, you have the option to run with the default setting of *Permit*, but the most secure is *Deny*.

Save File and URL History in the Player

This setting is used to allow Media Player to record a list of files you have recently opened. If you *Permit* this setting, another person using your copy of Media Player can immediately see what you have been viewing.

The default setting is *Permit* and the most secure is *Deny*.

Cookies

You can determine how cookies are used by your system from this screen, although this setting should really be considered in the wider context of Internet Explorer and how your privacy settings are configured for all online activity.

If you click on the Cookies button (shown in Figure 1-5) it will take you to the Internet Properties dialog box, normally accessed through Internet Explorer > Tools > Internet Options... under the Privacy tab.

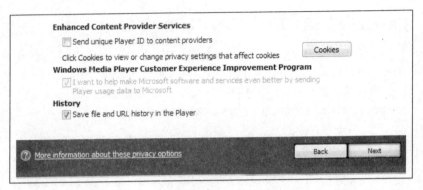

*Figure 1-5 To configure Cookie you need to use
Internet Explorer*

To read Microsoft's comprehensive statement
on how they are approaching privacy, you can
view the statement on the website at:

http://www.microsoft.com/windows/windowsm
edia/player/vista/privacy.aspx.

When you are satisfied, you have finished configuring
your privacy settings, click *Next* to continue.

Default Music and Video Player

Figure 1-6 shows the next screen in the setup routine.

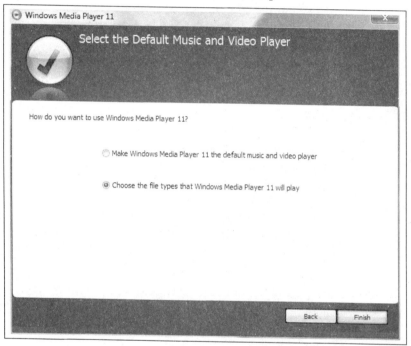

Figure 1-6 You can instruct Media Player to be responsible for a subset or all of your content

From this screen, you can opt either to allow Media Player to take over the role of playing all digital content it understands (and this covers a wide variety of formats), or if you would prefer, use a third party product for some media files and Media Player for others (third party products include Real Player and Sonic can be installed alongside Media Player 11).

If you select the topmost option, *Make Windows Media Player 11 the default music and video player*, all digital music and video content on your PC is played using Media Player.

> If file associations for other players existed, such as for .avi files or .mp3 files, this option will remove the old association and associate those file types with Media Player. In future, running the content from the Windows Explorer (double-clicking it) will automatically fire up Media Player.

If, on the other hand, you want to use your other media player software for specific file types, you should select *Choose the file types that Windows Media Player 11 will play* then click *Finish*.

This automatically fires up the *Set associations for a program* screen (shown in Figure 1-7) where you should tick each of the file types you want Media Player to be responsible for.

Do not forget to save your selection when you are done.

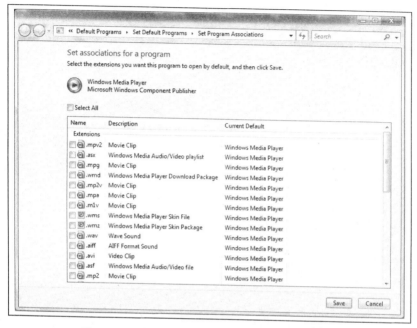

Figure 1-7 Select the file types that Media Player will automatically be responsible for playing

Even if you opt to not set Media Player as the default player for a specific file type, for example all .mp3 files, you can still have Media Player play these files by simply pressing Ctrl + O then locating the file in the file system through the file browser and clicking Open.

When you have saved you selection, the window will close and you will have your first view of what Media Player looks like. If you want to adjust any of the settings you've entered during the setup process you can do this using the Welcome Center.

> In Vista, you can access the Welcome Center through the Start button, selecting *All Programs* then *Accessories* then *Welcome Center*. Click on *Windows Media Player Set up* then press *Start* (located in the top right of the Welcome Center).

2

The Interface

The Media Player interface is built using Vista technology, although capable of running on Windows XP, and like most other Vista products, this interface is significantly improved over previous iterations to make it more ergonomically acceptable and easier to navigate.

To make this possible, a lot of the underlying power of the player is hidden beneath the menu system, leaving the main interface, shown in Figure 2-1, purely for finding, playing and manipulating your digital content.

Starting at the top of the screen and working down, we'll take a look at each of the components that comprise the interface.

Figure 2-1 The new Media Player interface is optimised for searching through the library

Firstly, the crossbar menu at the top of the screen, as with other Vista applications (if you are using Vista), is where you control what is displayed in the main window (directly beneath the crossbar) and where you switch primary functionality from one thing to another.

Each button on this crossbar menu is split into two parts. The topmost part switches the main screen to the capability shown on that button. However, if you try hovering the mouse over the bottom of the button, you will immediately see a highlighted arrow that allows you to view a drop-down menu of options for that capability. For example, if you drop down the options menu for the *Library* capability, you'll see options for creating playlists, selecting genres and adding music to your library.

The buttons on the crossbar are as follows:

- Now Playing
- Library
- Rip
- Burn
- Sync
- Online Stores.

What's Playing?

The *Now Playing* tab is by far the most straightforward of the Media Player interfaces to understand, and it's a great place to start.

If you switch to the *Now Playing* tab, by default you will see one of the many visualizations available through the drop-down menu (for example, *Now Playing* then *Visualizations* then *Battery* then *cottonstar*).

If you click on Download Visualizations (in the Visualizations submenu of Now Playing) Media Player launches Internet Explorer then directs you to the Microsoft

Media Player Visualizations web page where there are plenty of custom-made visualizations to choose.

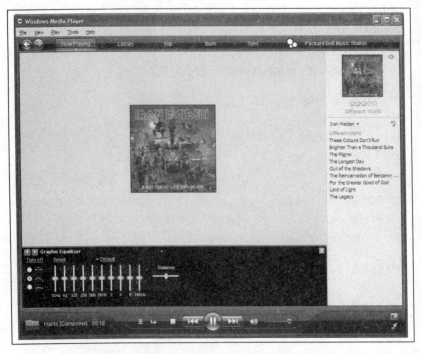

*Figure 2-2 Use the Graphic Equalizer to best
adjust the sound output for your speakers*

Follow the online instruction for installing and optimizing the visualization to suit your Media Player needs.

If you click on *Show Enhancements* (in the *Now Playing* sub-menu, see Figure 2-2), a graphic equalizer appears at the bottom of the main screen.

From the Microsoft Media Player you can download custom skins (custom look and feel interfaces for Media Player), extra visualizations developed either by Microsoft or third-party vendors, as well as plug-ins to add functionality to Media Player.

You can use the graphic equalizer as you would a physical graphic equalizer on a typical hi-fi component, adjusting balance and level for each of the ten available frequency ranges.

If you click on the small arrows in the top left-hand corner of the display, you can scroll through a full set of interfaces that allow you to adjust the playback speed (great for speeding up speech broadcasts such as podcasts or audio books when the speaker might be talking too slowly for your liking) and you can also switch on Media Player's *quiet mode*, whereby frequency suppression compresses the sound to make the average volume of the output more consistent.

A further enhancement, called *SRS WOW Effects*, introduces an integrated technology that introduces audio enhancement techniques that allow you to scale your audio output to suit your physical speaker arrangement and boost your system's bass representation to your output device, see Figure 2-3.

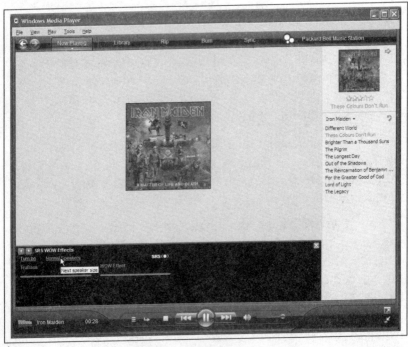

*Figure 2-3 Use the SRS WOW Effects to adjust
the overall sound performance for your
speakers*

For more information on SRS WOW and how it integrates with Media Player, take a look at http://mediaplayer.srswowcast.com.

The *Video Settings* (shown in Figure 2-4) enhancement menu lets you adjust the hue, saturation, brightness and contrast of video played in Media Player and is really useful in adjusting home movies or video that is not represented that well on the PC.

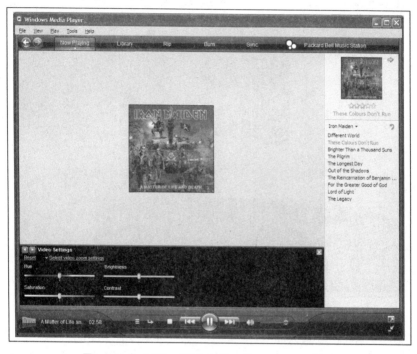

*Figure 2-4 Use Video Settings controls to
control video colour attributes for playback*

Crossfading and Auto Volume Levelling allows you to add a fade out/fade in effect between items in your playlist, and, as its name suggests, Auto Volume Levelling allows Media Player to have consistent playback volume even if the source content output level changes from one track to the next, see Figure 2-5.

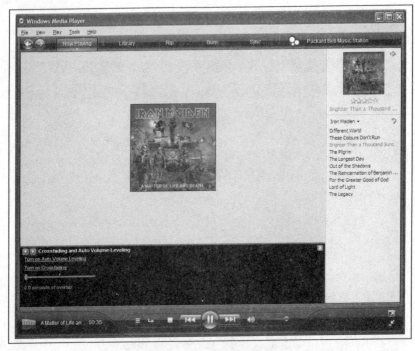

Figure 2-5 Add blending effects between tracks

Notice also that the List Pane (on the right-hand side of Media Player when using the Now Playing view) contains a list of all tracks to be played in the current playlist.

If you have selected a single track to play directly from the library, you'll see all the tracks in the library that follow the current, playing track.

The List Pane can be switched off from the Now Playing drop-down menu.

You can select a new track to start playing from the List Pane by double-clicking on the track.

Beneath the List Pane, there are two small blue buttons:

- Full screen
- Switch to skin mode.

Selecting the full screen view, allows Media Player to take over the entire screen, removing toolbars, the start menu and task bars. This is a mode for party playing on a big screen while entertaining.

To revert back to a windowed view, press Escape or move the mouse (to reveal the task bar at the bottom of the screen) and click the blue button on the bottom right-hand corner of the screen entitled *Exit full-screen mode*.

At the bottom of the screen there is a common set of controls which you'll recognise across many of the Vista applications, buttons that represent, play/pause, stop, next and previous tracks, repeat and shuffle, see Figure 2-6.

Figure 2-6 The standard tool bar offers quick access to the most common playback controls

If you switch on shuffle, the order of the songs played from your library will be random. If you click the shuffle button again a second time, the player will revert to playing the tracks in order as presented in the library. Turning on repeat will force a replay of the track you are currently listening to.

If you select *Now Playing* then *Plug-ins* then *Download Plug-ins*, you will be redirected to the Microsoft Media Player website where you can download new functionality to augment Media Player's capabilities.

This site contains downloads of DVD decoder software, new MP3 encoders and Media Player powertoys and utilities, such as new auto-playlists.

To really get under the hood of Media Player, download TweakMP. This powertoy (capable of working on all Media Player editions from Version 9) enables you to get into all the hidden Medial Player settings, whereby you obtain total control over everything Media Player could possible be configured to do.

Finally, under *Now Playing* then *Plug-Ins* then *Options...* you can alter the properties (where possible) of installed plug-ins and visualisations.

The options dialog box is used to perform much of the advanced media player configuration covered later.

3

The Media Library

The *Library* is the main screen for viewing and manipulating digital content. From this Library drop-down menu, you can create new playlists of content and switch the view between music, pictures, video, recorded TV or miscellaneous content items (under the *other* heading), see Figure 3-1.

Each of the categories of content type, such as music or pictures, will focus the display on the library containing content of that nature. By default, the user's profile directories, such as your own music and pictures folders, will be displayed, however, you can add files to the library from other folders (or network locations) and these will all be shown as one consolidated library resource in Media Player.

On the left-hand side of the screen, you will see two top-level folders called *Playlists* and *Library*. This is called the *Navigation Pane*.

Figure 3-1 The Library is where you'll control most of what you do in Media Player

Playlists are predefined lists of songs that you can select to play as an ordered list. There is more detail on using, creating and deleting playlists later in this chapter, but for now, you can click on the preinstalled playlists (such as all music) to see how it presents information in the library.

The *Library* folders are used to change what is displayed in the main view on the right-hand side of the screen – each option changing the content displayed in library view.

Figure 3-2. Use the categories on the left to determine how your library appears

Selecting *Songs*, beneath the *Library* menu option, displays every album and track listing (this is the default view). Alternatively, to aid you in searching for a specific album or artist, selecting *Album* will display the cover art of all your albums in alphabetical order oriented around the album name, while selecting *Artist* will display the cover art for all albums in alphabetical order oriented around the artist's name, (see Figure 3-2).

Above the *Navigation Pane*, there are three overhead drop-down menus running from left to right. Each drop-down menu controls what is displayed in the library view, with each item to the right being more specific in grouping that category than the previous.

Figure 3-3 Use the menu bar at the top to configure the view in the main library window

If you select *Music* then *Library* then *Album* you will see all your album art shown in the library in alphabetical order (see Figure 3-3). Selecting *Video* then *Library* then *Folder* will display all your library folders that contain video items, again in alphabetical order oriented around the folder name, see Figure 3-4.

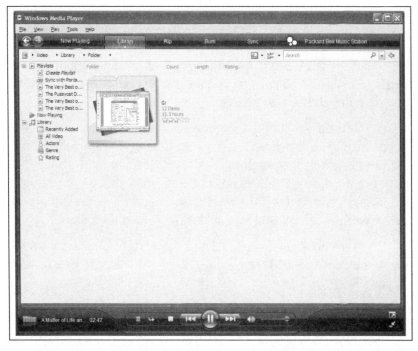

Figure 3-4 Order the view to see which video folders your system is monitoring

The search box to the upper right-hand side of the screen allows you to perform very fast interactive searches of your entire library using media information known as metadata.

> Metadata is used extensively in Vista (less so in Windows XP) to help users of applications better manipulate and categorise data files for use in the real world. Date, time, tagging information and star ratings are all forms of metadata that are used in Media Player.

You can search on any textual information associated with your digital content, such as album name, artist's name or the date the album was released.

If you've added extra tagging information about the track using the *Advanced Tag Editor* you can search on additional track information you've added yourself about the artist, song lyrics, pictures associated with the track, or any additional comments you might have added, for example a review of the album that you sent in to Amazon.co.uk.

To start the Advanced Tag Editor, right-click on a track then select Advanced Tag Editor from the context menu, see Figure 3-5.

Figure 3-5. Use the Advanced Tag Editor to add additional information in to your library

To the left of the search box there are two drop-down boxes worth discussing. The leftmost of these offers a number of options for changing the layout of the screen (*Layout Options*), allowing you to toggle on and off the *Navigation Pane* and the *List Pane*, add the classic menu bar to this version of Media Player to align it with previous versions (File, View, Play, Tools and Help), and modify the columns displayed at the top of the library screen.

Between the *Layout Options* menu and the search box is the *View Options* menu. Using this menu, you can change the library layout to show a detailed view (with no album art), a less detailed view with album art (the default) or if you prefer, only an icon.

Use the arrow to the right of the search box to expose the *List Pane* if it has previously been hidden, see Figure 3-6.

Figure 3-6 Use the List Pane to create playlists

The Media Player controls at the bottom of the screen are consistent throughout each of the menu tabs and always perform the same functions (play/pause, stop, next/previous track, repeat, shuffle and volume up and down).

Content Format Types

Using the library interface you can search for a variety of different content types: music, videos, recorded TV and various other types of uncategorised content.

Figure 3-7 View different content types with one click of the Library drop-down menu

Changing from one form of digital content to another is as easy as dropping down the *Library* menu and selecting the appropriate content library you are interested in from the list, see Figure 3-7.

Music, pictures and video are fairly self-explanatory, with the default file locations being in your user's profile under the *Pictures*, *Music* and *Videos* folders.

More interesting maybe (and certainly new to many users), recorded TV shows that have been recorded in the Microsoft Recorded TV Show format (files ending with the extension .dvr-ms) can now be played directly through this interface without having to run Media Center.

> If you have Windows XP Media Center 2005 or one of the Media Center Vista platforms you can simply point Media Player directly at the recorded TV show files in your profile.

If you have Media Center running on the same computer as you are running Media Player, the files are automatically recorded in your user profile and can be played straight back using either Media Center or, if you are working and want them shrunk into a small window, you can view them in Media Player.

Furthermore, if you want to take recorded TV shows with you on a machine not capable of running Media Center, simply copy the files from the Media Center computer (using removable media or a wireless or wired network) and put them in your profile's *Recorded TV* folder.

The *Other* category is to use for files that do not fall into any of the categories already discussed. These might be digital media files that rely on a proprietary codec to play them, or perhaps you wish to store files that you have paid for and licensed using DRM in this separate category.

Creating and Using Playlists

Playlists are collections of digital media that you have grouped together for a specific purpose, such as songs for a themed party, driving music or classical music for the mother-in-law.

Another great reason for creating playlists is that a playlist can be used to synchronise content with a portable media player, for example, you can create a synchronisation with a media device with less memory than your hard drive, synchronising only a select few tracks to suit your listening needs.

Playlists are easy to create, using either the *Library* drop-down menu and selecting *Create Playlist* or, to shortcut the menu clicks, press Ctrl + N. This will expose the *List Pane* on the right-hand side of the screen and offer you a blank playlist with the name: *Untitled Playlist*, see Figure 3-8.

The first thing to do is rename the playlist to something more meaningful. Click on the arrow next to the playlist name to expose the drop-down menu and select *Rename Playlist*. To add tracks to the playlist, it's a simple matter of dragging them from the library view into the List Pane where it says *Drag items here.*

Figure 3-8 Give the new playlist a meaningful name

Once you are happy with the selection of songs in your playlist, you can right-click on any song shown in the *List Pane* and use the context menu items *Remove from List*, *Move Up* and *Move Down*, to delete that track, or change the play order.

When you are happy with the contents of your playlist and its order of play, click the *Save Playlist* at the bottom of the *List Pane*.

Your playlist will have an extension of .*wpl* and will, by default, be stored in the *My Playlists* folder in your profile under the *Music* folder.

To view all playlists you have stored on your system, or select a playlist for use, use the *Playlists* menu in the Navigation Pane, expanding *Playlists* then selecting the one you recently saved from the tree, see Figure 3-9.

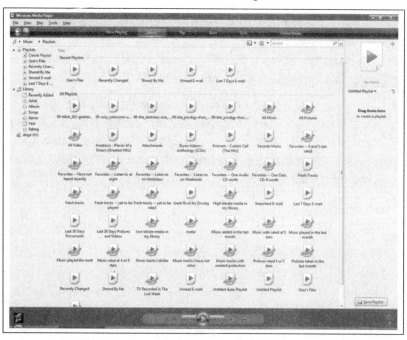

Figure 3-9 Select a playlist from the list pane

There will already be a set of playlists created by default on your system, based on criteria such as when the files were added to your library, their star rating and favourites (based on the number of times the track has been listened to).

> It is worth noting that you can create playlists of photos, video and TV all using the same technique. This is important since portable media devices are now capable of playing so much more than simple MP3 music files.

Auto playlists are even more useful, dynamically updating themselves from metadata associated with items in your library. Auto playlists use rules to determine membership, and these rules are extremely flexible.

To create an auto playlist, drop down the *Library* menu then select *Create Auto Playlist*. In the dialog box, shown in Figure 3-10, give the auto playlist a meaningful name then proceed to create the rules that automatically populate that playlist with content.

Figure 3-10 Use auto playlists to add content automatically from your library based on set search criteria

To create a rule in an auto playlist you will need to do the following:

1. Click on the green cross under the topmost item in the rules list, *Music in my library*. This will open the *criteria* drop-down menu box and offer an initial selection of 20

criteria to choose from (although there are more available if you select More... at the bottom of the list). Choose the criterion that best matches the content you want to include in this playlist, such as *Genre*.

2. You will see the *Genre* criterion listed as *Genre Is [click to set]* (notice the *is* is actually underlined). Click on this *is* to change the logic being applied by this operand, selecting: *is*, *is not* or *contains*. In this example of *Genre* you might use *contains* if you wanted all rock music, but there were many genres associated with rock, for example, soft rock, heavy rock, glam rock, etc. If you are planning to create the playlist by exclusion, you can use *is not* as the operand and, in the genre example, exclude all dance music.

3. When you have set the operand, click on *[click to set]* and select the item from the drop-down list that matches your requirement, for example, in the case of *genre*, you might select *Blues*.

4. To add more criteria to the list, you can add as many of these rules as you like. You might start by creating a genre rule, then add another rule for the *Release Year*. In this way you could start building up a playlist of '80s Soul music, for example.

5. Use the *And also include:* criteria to include other content types into the playlist, such as music, pictures and video.

6. Finally, add a restriction to the playlist if required, such as a maximum number of tracks, or a size limit. This is particularly useful if you are using this playlist as the one

you synchronise with a portable device with limited space, see Figure 3-11.

Figure 3-11 Add device restrictions to the auto playlist to limit the number of content items

7. When you have added all the criteria necessary to filter your library the way you want, click OK. This adds the new playlist to the list in the *Navigation Pane*.

From now on when new music is added to your library, if it meets the criteria specified by the rules in the playlist, Media Player automatically makes those tracks members of that playlist. Each time you synchronise with a portable device, the updated playlist is automatically transferred to the remote device.

Adding Content to the Library

To add new digital content into your library there are two methods.

- You can manually copy the content into your default library, such as the Music folder in your profile
- You can connect a new device (or create a new folder) on your PC and add the folder path to the Monitored Folders list to force Media Player to look in that new folder each time it starts.

If you add multiple albums from a single artist to your library, Media Player will start stacking the items in the library so that when you view them by artist, you immediately see how many albums by this artist you have.

To access the interface for configuring how content is added to the Media Player monitored folders list, click in the *Library* drop-down menu and select *Add to library…*

You will see the screen shown in Figure 3-12. Make sure are select *Advanced Options* to view the list of monitored folders.

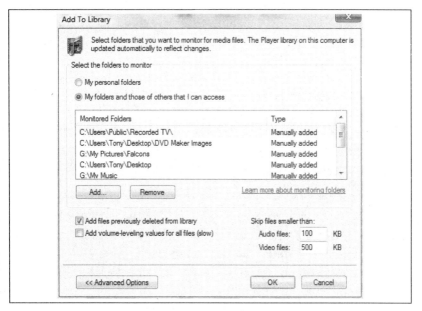

Figure 3-12 To add new folders to the monitored list, use the Advanced Options

You can add or remove folders from the list using the Add and Remove buttons. Folders can be local to your computer, or they can exist on another PC accessible over your network.

In the case of a folder which is under the control of another user or PC, that folder will need access rights that allow you to connect to and read the content before you can use it.

If you check the checkbox stating *Add files previously deleted from my library,* Media Player will automatically enter content back into the library if you have previously deleted the entry.

Adding files back into the library if they have been removed is only possible if the file still exists on your hard disc. If you physically delete the file rather than just the library entry, Media Player cannot recover it from the recycle bin.

If you want to apply volume levelling to the tracks as they are imported into your library, the time taken to integrate each track takes much longer since each track's volume is assessed against an average then the track is suppressed or enhanced to align it with that average.

You can also stop Media Player from incorporating audio and video files beneath a certain threshold. This is particularly useful for stopping fragments of songs and video being imported into your library and cluttering it up.

Library Sharing (Vista Only)

Sharing data and collaborating is a common theme when you look across the set of applications delivered with the Vista product set, no less so in Media Player context.

If you have a home network with more than one PC on it, you can share a Media Player library from a single location, or you can choose to distribute the files across multiple libraries across any number of PCs and have open access to each shared library on your network.

A network makes sharing your content really easy, with all the extra benefits of being able to consume content from any location your network reaches.

> PCs trying to use *Library Sharing* must be part of the same physical network, connected with IP addresses in the same subnet. Library Sharing cannot be used in a Windows domain environment (a business network).

If you want to set up sharing, drop down the *Library* menu and select *Library Sharing....* Check the *Share my library* checkbox then click OK.

When you click OK, you will see an expanded dialog box showing the same options as before, only the dialog is now augmented with a list of network devices available for sharing.

Right-click on any of the devices shown in the window to configure how they will be shared on the network.

It is possible to set up library sharing on your system without using the Media Player menu system. However, you will have to configure your firewall settings to permit the following TCP ports, all with a defined scope in the local subnet: 554, 2177, 2869, 10243. You will also need to open the following UDP ports, again with a scope of local subnet only: 1900, 2177, 5004-5005, 10280-10284.

Each device can be configured in a different way if you require, using the *Allow privilege to authorise access* or the *Deny privilege to block access*.

You can disable or remove the device if you do not want it included in your network sharing profile.

More granular control over the information that can be shared is possible if you click on the *Settings...* button.

Sharing content grants any network user access to your content. Consider if you want this to happen before allowing sharing to be used.

Album Art and Media Information

If you want Media Player to check the Internet for updates of media information, including album art and track listings, you can use the option in the Library drop-down menu entitled *Apply Media Information Changes*, see Figure 3-13.

Figure 3-13 Add metadata obtained from the Internet to your library

Adding metadata from the Internet can be quite a slow process as Media Player must check each track and album identifier contained in your library against an online database. If it finds new information, this must be downloaded to your computer and paired up with the media content files.

If you have a large media library with a lot of untagged content, you should be aware that this process may take up to a few hours to complete.

Advanced Library Options

There are a few more options you need to be aware of for configuring how Media Player handles the information contained within your library and how media files are kept or deleted, depending on your preferences.

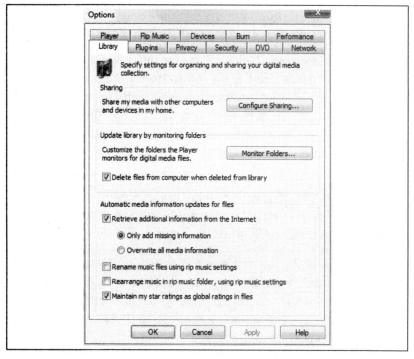

Figure 3-14 Use the Library Options tab to configure advanced library options

To access the advanced options for your media library, click on the *Library* drop-down menu and select *More Options...* This will open the Options dialog box shown in Figure 3-14.

By default the checkbox *Delete files from computer when deleted from library* is selected. This means when you right-click on a track in the library and select delete, the file is sent to the recycle bin. If, however, you would prefer to delete the track from the library but keep the source content file on the hard disc, you should uncheck this checkbox.

It's also a good idea, if you want to keep files on the hard disc but don't want them in the library, to move them to another location that is not automatically scanned as a monitored folder. In this way you can permit the monitored folders functionality to automatically add in all files it finds in monitored folders without having to toggle that setting on and off.

Further configuration items at the bottom of the dialog box allow you to override Internet information downloaded for a file using settings predefined as specific *rip music* settings.

> By default, the settings for overriding Internet acquired metadata are not checked by default since most people are happy to use Internet supplied information as it tends to be effortless and mostly accurate.

You can also instruct Media Player to always update the entire library's metadata set rather than just look at new files.

> Be warned, updating the entire library can take a very long time and should only be done when you don't need to do anything else with Media Player for a few hours.

4

Ripping Content

Ripping music to your library is easier now than ever before with Media Player 11, with the most important update being that of making the settings more accessible and easy to understand to the user.

You'll notice when you select the *Rip* tab, that it instructs you to begin with, to insert an audio CD into the CD drive.

Before you begin, drop down the *Rip* menu to see how easy it is to change the file formats and bit rates that tracks can be ripped to, see Figure 4-1.

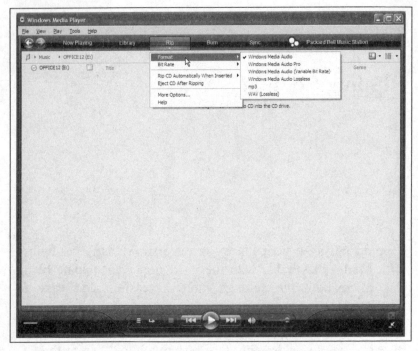

*Figure 4-1 The menu system for ripping CDs
makes finding settings extremely easy*

There are six file formats you can choose from but the most versatile and cross-platform capable of these is certainly MP3. Nevertheless, Media Player defaults to the Microsoft proprietary format of Windows Media Audio. If you are using a portable media device that plays MP3s, be sure to switch the file format before you begin ripping CDs to your library, otherwise you will have to re-rip or convert the tracks to MP3 in the future.

The bit rate is the rate at which the digital sample of the original CD is copied to its new ripped file format. When deciding on the best bit rate to suit your system, a balance must be struck between the quality you require and the file size of the ripped track.

The default bit rate in Media Player is 128 Kbps, offering a good halfway compromise with relatively small files and virtually undetectable loss on the original track's CD quality.

If, however, you are a connoisseur of music and demand the best quality available, you can switch the bit rate to sample at 192 Kbps, giving you a virtually lossless conversion to the new file format. On the other hand, to preserve disc space or to fit more tracks on a portable device with limited memory you can compromise on quality for the smallest file size and select 48 Kbps.

If you want to speed up the ripping process, cutting down on the number of mouse clicks needed to start the process, you can follow the *Rip* menu item *Rip CD Automatically When Inserted* and select *Always*. This option will start the ripping process immediately as you insert a CD into the drive, even if Media Player is not focused on the *Rip* tab. The default setting is to start automatically if you are focused on the Rip tab.

Lastly, there is an option to never start automatically, rather you have to click the Rip [album name] item in the *Rip* menu or click the *Start Rip* button in the bottom right-hand corner of the interface.

If you want the CD automatically ejected from the CD drive when it has been copied to your library, select the *Eject CD After Ripping* menu item from the *Rip* menu. If you are ripping a lot of music, this can be a great reminder that the rip has completed and it's time to put in the next disc. In this case you might want to have the system start ripping automatically when you put a new CD in the drive also.

> Before you start ripping CDs, you will have to decide how you will be handling copy protection. Media Player allows you to protect the music you rip to ensure that you don't infringe any copyright law if your media files end up finding their way into the public domain. Nevertheless, be warned, that copy protection will prohibit your media being played on other devices that you own, and this is perfectly acceptable within the bounds of the law. Whatever you decide, you will have to check the disclaimer checkbox, thereby absolving Microsoft of any copy protection or copyright infringement as a result of your own misuse of the digital content.

Select whether or not you wish to use copy protection to your music and check the disclaimer before clicking OK. You should now see the track listing and the album information in the Rip interface, and as each track is copied to your library, you'll see a notification that it is *Ripped to library*.

A progress bar is shown for each track as it is ripped, see Figure 4-2.

Figure 4-2 Watch the progress as tracks are copied one at a time to your library

Advanced Ripping Options

Take a look in the Options dialog box for the Rip function (drop down the *Rip* menu then select *More Options*), as shown in Figure 4-3.

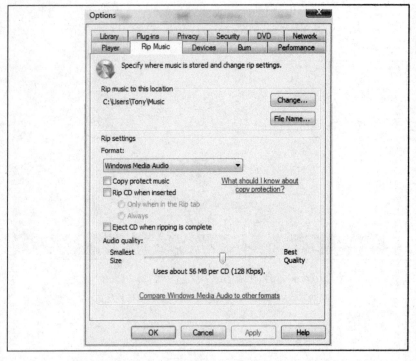

Figure 4-3 Use the Options dialog to change advanced ripping settings

You can change the default location where new music is ripped to, the default being the Music folder in your user profile (C:\Users\<username>\Music).

To change the file location click the *Change...* button in the *Options* dialog box under the *Rip Music* tab.

You can alter the way the file name for each track is created, using different metadata information available when the track is found on the online information services.

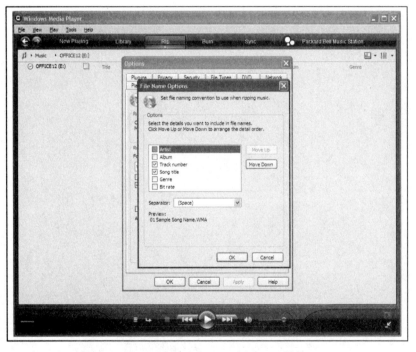

Figure 4-4 Adjust the automatic file name generation settings to suit your own library

Click on *File Name...* to see the full list of information that can be used to create the file name for ripped music, see Figure 4-4.

5

Creating CDs

Creating (also know as burning) CDs using Media Player is really easy. Click on the *Burn* interface tab and drop down the menu to see the options available for CD creation, see Figure 5-1.

If you have not inserted a blank CD that is writable using Vista, you will see a message in the main interface window stating *To begin, insert a blank disc into the drive.*

*Figure 5-1 Creating your own CDs is easy
using Media Player 11*

You have the option of creating two distinctly different kinds of CD:

- An audio CD for playing in a standard CD player

- A data CD containing exact copies of the source files, such as your MP3s.

If you opt to create a data CD, you will effectively be doing a straightforward copy of the files that exist in your library to the CD.

Alternatively, creating an audio CD forces the reformatting of the source files into the appropriate format necessary to be played on a normal CD player. As this file format is substantially larger than the MP3 format, for example, you'll find that while 50 MP3s might fit easily on a data CD, only 18 tracks will fit onto the audio CD.

It's worth checking to see if the CD player supports MP3. If this is the case, you can create a data CD of MP3s that are playable by the CD player.

The first thing to do when you want to create a new CD is to place the blank CD in the CD writer.

Figure 5-2 Media Player informs you how much space is available on your CD

Media Player will automatically recognise a new blank CD and report its availability through the user interface in the list pane in the top right corner of the screen, see Figure 5-2.

In the *List Pane* on the right-hand side, you'll see the *Burn List* initially with no items in it, see Figure 5-3.

Figure 5-3 Drag library items into the list pane to create the burn list

The *Burn List* is where you add tracks you wish to be written to the CD. The trick for using the *Burn List* is to switch back to the *Library* tab and find the music you want to burn.

Next, click back to the *Burn* tab and start dragging the tracks you are interested in over to the *Burn List*, see Figure 5-4.

Figure 5-4 Add tracks from the Library to the
Burn List by dragging them across to the right

To select multiple tracks from the library, hold down the Ctrl key and click successively on each track you want copied to the CD. When you have selected a group of tracks, release the Ctrl key then drag any of them to the burn list.

As you drag each track to the CD, Media Player reports back how much space is left to copy more files. When you are ready to commit the tracks to the CD, click the *Burn* menu item on the *Burn* menu, or click the *Start Burn* button in the bottom right-hand corner of the main interface. This will take a little time, so be patient.

Progress is shown as a green progress bar beside each of the track names, see Figure 5-5.

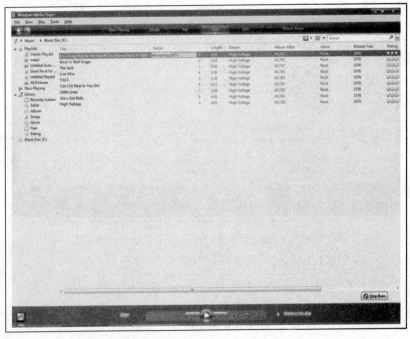

Figure 5-5 Burning a CD can take time but you can still use Media Player to play other tracks

Advanced Burning Option

If you access the Options dialog box for advanced burning settings, you will see the dialog box shown in Figure 5-6.

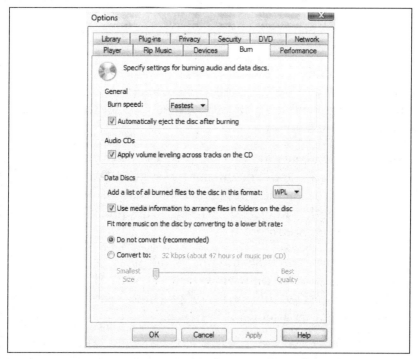

Figure 5-6 There are a variety of advanced options to configure how CDs are created

It is very rare that you would ever have to change the burn speed from its default of *Fastest*, however, if you are experiencing problems with the CDs you are creating, it is a good way of testing whether or not the writer is experiencing a technical fault.

> If the problem is fixed by reducing the speed the burn is working at, it might be that there is a hardware fault with the drive that needs repairing.

Selecting *Automatically eject the disk after burning* speaks for itself, but it's worth remembering that the option is there to be switched off in case you don't want the CD taken offline once it's created.

> Some people like sharing their CD drive on the network, and this might be a good way of quickly sharing information with others on your network without going through the process of *Library Sharing*.

Volume levelling will ensure all tracks on your newly created CD have the same audio output levels. This makes for a consistent level in the playback, something which is essential for a comfortable listening experience.

Data CDs are always copied with an associated playlist, either in WPL (standard Media Player playlist format) or in M3U (a standard MP3 playlist format). This means that another media player, capable of using playlists, can exploit this data and display it on its own interface.

If you allow Media Player to arrange the files according to the metadata in your library, the files will be stored in folders ordered by the artists name then the album name and finally the track. If you clear the checkbox for using media information, all files will be stored in the root folder of the data CD.

Lastly, you can adjust the bit rate for the copied files to fit more of these files onto the destination CD. In this way, you can keep high quality files on your PC, yet write low quality files to your CD to maximise its capacity to hold more tracks.

6

Synchronising with Portable Devices

As soon as you connect a Media Center compatible portable device to your PC (be it Vista or Windows XP), Media Player can be configured to automatically synchronize playlists with it, copying whatever tracks you predetermine should be copied across.

Firstly, however, you need to go through a short configuration process for that device before it becomes an automatic capability.

The very first time you connect a portable device to your system, you will be presented with a dialog box that allows you to authorise Media Player to govern that device, hence overwriting any existing files on the device or leaving any existing files intact and augmenting them with new files from your library, see Figure 6-1.

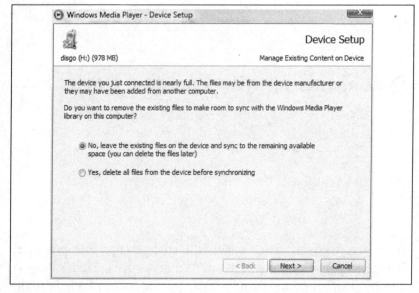

*Figure 6-1 The first time you connect a device
you can ask Media Player to wipe it clean*

When you are shopping around for portable media device that will seamlessly integrate with Media Player 11, make sure to look for the *PlaysForSure* (see Appendix) logo on the hardware you invest in. This logo is Microsoft's seal of approval on devices that have been tested and authorised as fully compliant with Media Player.

If you are happy to overwrite the files on the portable device, select *Yes, delete all files from the device before synchronizing* then click *Next*.

Next, you are asked to confirm whether or not you are happy for Media Center to delete any content on the device (last chance to save your data). Clicking *Yes* will delete everything on that device and leave it fresh and clean for synchronizing with your Media Center library.

Finally, you are asked to name your portable device. Choose a name that is meaningful to you then click on *Finish*.

The first time a new device is connected to Media Player (one that is new to Media Player that is, not necessarily one that is just out of the plastic carton) Media Player will select what it feels is the best way of synchronizing with that device, either automatically or manually. If your portable device has enough memory to hold an entire copy of your library, Media Player will synchronize with it automatically, copying everything over. If the capacity of the drive is lesser than that of your library, Media Player reverts to a manual mode allowing you to select which songs and playlists are transferred. When you click *Finish* in the device setup routine, Media Player selects the synchronization mode, either starting the sync automatically or passing control to you to do it manually.

When the device set-up routine finishes, you can switch to the *Sync* tab to see the device shown in the List Pane on the right of the library. You'll see an icon representing the device and some information about the device's capacity and how much space is left to copy data onto it. If the device cannot be detected by Media Center you will see the screen shown in Figure 6-2 when you click on the *Sync* tab. Note that the message in the top right-hand corner of the screen states *Connect a device*.

Figure 6-2 If your device is not recognised by Media Player, it will ask you to Connect a device

Shuffling Music

A great feature of this latest version of Media Player is the ability to shuffle content onto the device.

You can shuffle content using either the *click here* link on the *List Pane*, or through the *Sync* drop-down menu where you select, *Shuffle [device name]*.

Figure 6-3 Media Player sends a whole set of new tracks to the device each time you shuffle

When you select *Shuffle,* Media Player will copy a random selection of track onto the device to fill its capacity. This is great for MP3 players with limited space, say, 1 GB of memory where your library is an order of magnitude greater.

Each time you select the *Shuffle* option, Media Player will replace the files on your device with a whole set of new ones.

During the process where Media Player synchronizes with your mobile media device, you will see the progress mapped out as shown in Figure 6-3.

Setting up Synchronizations

To get down into the details of setting up clever and customised synchronization regimes for each of your portable devices, drop down the *Sync* menu, select the device's name from the menu then select *Set Up Sync...*This opens the Device Setup screen shown in Figure 6-4.

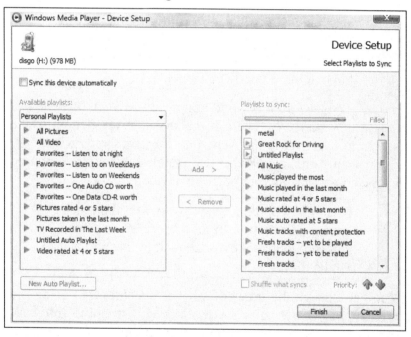

Figure 6-4 Select custom playlists to auto sync with small capacity portable devices

If your system is currently set to manually synchronize your device due to capacity constraints, you can instruct Media Player to switch to automatically synchronize with whichever playlists you want.

> The real trick to making this work is to use auto playlists that you have developed rules specifically for being applicable to your being 'on the road'. You can easily create a custom auto playlist that contains rules to limit the size of the playlist it creates. Remember the constraints you can build into auto playlists at the bottom of the filters screen.

To make all this work, you need to switch on *Sync this device automatically*. There is a shortcut at the bottom of the screen to take you to the *New Auto Playlist* screen where you can instantly create a playlist that matches the criteria imposed by the constraints of your portable device.

> Double-click on a playlist to see the tracks contained within it. In the *View Playlist* screen, you can double-click on a track to listen to it in Media Player.

You can change the order of what is synchronized using the priority arrows beneath *Playlists to sync* list and if you want the songs to shuffle when they arrive on the device, select the checkbox *Shuffle what syncs*.

Click Finish when you are done.

When you exit from setting up the sync, Media Player will start synchronizing automatically with your device.

Advanced Options for Portable Devices

There are two places where you can access advanced options for synchronizing your portable devices; through the *Sync* dropdown menu, selecting the device name then *Advanced Options* where you specify options for each individual device, and through the normal *Options* dialog where you specify option for the Media Player end of the synchronization.

Firstly we will take a look at the *Advanced Options* dialog box, particular to this functionality of each individual portable device. Click on *Sync* then select your *[device name]* then select *Advanced Options...*

The properties dialog box here is specifically for this device.

You'll see the synchronization name for this device (by default this is the same as the device name as recognised when you first plugged it into your computer) which you can change if you so desire.

If you check the checkbox *Create folder hierarchy on device* the synchronization will use library metadata, such as the artists name and album names to create a folder hierarchy on the device much in the same way as you would in your library or when you create a data CD.

If you want all the tracks copied to the root directory of your device, uncheck this box. You might wonder why you would ever want to synchronize into the root directory of your device without folders; however there are some devices around that require this. For example, some FM transmitter devices – the sort you use to transmit from an MP3 player to your car radio system – that allow you to plug in memory sticks with no real playback capability of their own. Although this is particularly useful and a cost effective way of taking music with you on the go, they only have simple, play, next/previous track and stop controls. There is no way to navigate folders and you get no clever display.

You can choose to start the synchronization as soon as the device connects or wait until you press the *Start Sync* button. The default for *Start sync when device connect* will depend on the initial set-up of that device – if the device has high capacity and can take your entire library it will be set to automatic, otherwise it will be set to manual.

If the device is a picture storage device, you can ask Media Player to automatically delete pictures from that device once they have been transferred into your library. Select the *Delete pictures from device once copied to computer*. This stops you having to manually delete images from a digital camera, for example, after you have copied them into your library.

Finally, on this screen, you can ask Media Player to reserve some of the capacity of the portable device for use by other information. You might also use the device to back up your Documents folder or keep copies of other non-Media Player related data. Use the slider to change the percentage of the portable device that remains preserved for other use.

Now try switching to the *Quality* tab. It's advisable you leave the topmost checkbox, *Convert music, pictures, videos, and TV shows as required*, selected as default. This ensures that Media Player will make best efforts to make your content play on the portable device, even if this required a format change from .wma to .mp3 or a downgrade in quality.

You can also opt to for a downgrade of content based on the settings of the two sliders, applying to both music and video content.

When you are done, click on OK.

On the other side of the synchronization, you can configure some Media Player specific options using the main Media Player *Options* dialog box (*Sync* then *More Options...*), then on the *Devices* tab, click *Advanced* button to see the *File Conversion Options* box shown in Figure 6-5

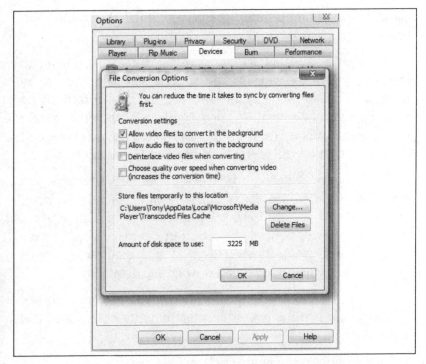

*Figure 6-5 Convert files before you start
synchronizing to speed things up*

Background conversion of files will occur for synchronization when the portable device is not plugged in.

Your system must also be idle (no user input from the keyboard or mouse) for at least 10 minutes before background conversion will begin.

If your portable device is plugged in, files are converted as the transfer happens, not in the background.

By default, background synchronization is enabled only for video files, but you can also switch it on for audio content as well if you so desire.

You can also instruct the conversion process to de-interlace video files on conversion (some media content players require this – you should look at the manufacturer's instructions for your device). Through this interface, you can improve the quality of converted video, change the folder used for temporary file conversions and specify the amount of temporary disc space used to hold the converted files.

The default upper limit of disc space that is utilised by the conversion process is 3225 MB but you might want to increase this if you have a lot of music and video to convert. At the end of the day, it is your call and is best optimised through trial and error.

You can use an Xbox 360 as a remote media player, using its built in media capability to connect to your shared library over your network. The Xbox 360 can also act as a Media Center Extender and can stream content from your Vista PC, over the wireless or wired network to anywhere it is connected to.

7

Buying Music Online

There are three kinds of content you can obtain from an online store:

- Free content
- Subscription content
- Purchased content.

Free content speaks for itself. This is downloadable content that comes with or without a licence, but whatever way it is copy protected, it is free to you.

Subscription content can either come at a cost, or be free also, but it is normally associated with regular updates of content, such as weekly radio shows, television shows or podcasts.

Purchased content comes at a premium and normally will be associated with a licence, which must also be downloaded to permit you to play the content.

A podcast is named after an iPod broadcast which is effectively an Internet radio show that can be downloaded to a portable media player, or streamed over the Internet.

When you click on the Online Stores tab you can access a massive variety of content provided through the online Windows Media interface, see Figure 7-1.

Figure 7-1 Access online content through the
Online Stores tab

Digital content (audio and video) can be sourced from a variety of online services and will be downloaded to your library in exactly the same way as ripped CD content.

The only difference between your ripped content and content sourced from an online service is that it might have Media Usage Rights for copy protection downloaded with it, limiting its use to your PC and prohibiting distribution.

As more and more content providers wake up to the new world order of digital content on the world wide web, new applications and plug-ins are changing the way we listen to and use digital content.

A good example of this is MTV's URGE service, see Figure 7-2.

URGE installs as a plug-in for both Media Player and Media Center and for a small subscription charge (paid monthly) much in the way you subscribe to a pay-per-view movie service, you have access to literally millions of audio tracks, music videos and other kinds of digital content. URGE also acts as a portal to a whole bunch of online radio channels that are free to connect and listen to. You can also opt to pay for and download tracks in the more traditional way. Whichever way you choose to use URGE, the integration of these technologies opens up the doors to a whole new way of viewing the digital world of multimedia content.

*Figure 7-2 MTV have an excellent online music
and radio service called URGE*

For more information on using URGE, or to download and install the URGE plug-in for Media Player, go to http://www.urge.com.

When you've successfully installed URGE on your system, you'll see a new URGE tab appear on the top menu crossbar where Online Stores was.

The Appendix at the end of this book looks in more detail at Online Media shops, the *PlaysForSure* badge and how you would go about ensuring that a portable media device would work correctly with Media Player.

8

Classic Media Player Menus

If you liked the way the menu system used to work in older versions of Media Player, never fear.

This *classic* menu bar containing *File*, *View*, *Play*, *Tools* and *Help* is accessed at any time by right-clicking on the blank space to the left of the *Now Playing* tab.

If you want to lock the classic menu onto the interface permanently, select *View* then select *Classic Menus*, see Figure 8-1.

You can toggle the *classic* menus on and off using the shortcut Ctrl + M.

Figure 8-1 Use the classic menus to operate
Media Player 11 like one of its predecessors

The classic menu offers options that align this new version of Media Player with its predecessors. This is convenient for those of us who fear change.

However, some functionality of the new player is not available any other way than through this classic menu system: namely, the Skin Chooser and skins download interface.

It is worth getting familiar with using both the new way of doing things and with using the classic menu where appropriate.

9

Using the Mini Player

At any time when you are using Media Player, you can minimise it so that a small version of the player docks onto your task bar, offering the same playback controls as before, but much more compact and unobtrusive on the rest of your desktop, see Figure 9-1. This is known as the Mini Player.

Figure9-1 The Mini Player offers controls similar to that of the main Media Player interface

In the bottom right-hand corner of the Mini Player, you will see the maximise icon used to return Media Player to its original size.

If you hover the mouse pointer over the Mini Player you see some additional information about the current track being played, and if you click the small icon above the maximise button, it switches on the Mini Player's Visualization window.

You can use the Mini Player visualizations pop-up to display a small video screen attached to the task bar when you are playing TV or video. In this way, you can watch video content without the player taking up any significant amount of your desktop.

10

Advanced Media Player

We will finish with a quick look at the options and settings available for best optimising the way Media Player operates in your environment.

> These settings are fairly advanced, so make sure you understand fully what you are doing before changing anything.

To get started, open the *More Options* dialog box shown in Figure 10-1 and click on the *Player* tab.

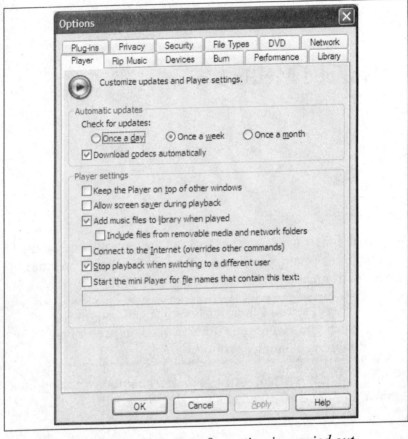

*Figure 10-1 Player configuration is carried out
using the Options dialog on the Player tab*

At the top of the page you can select how often Media
Player checks the online update service for software updates.

Available options are:

- Once a day

- Once a week

- Once a month.

Media Player software updates will undoubtedly appear occasionally.

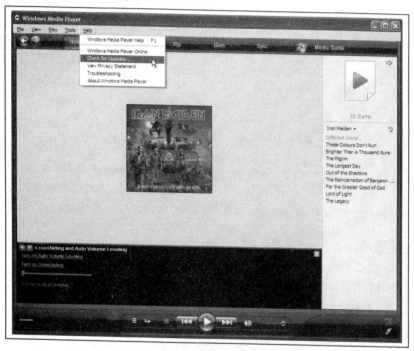

Figure 10-2 Download Media Player software updates automatically

You will probably find that setting *Once a month* is more than acceptable and if there is some specific update you hear about online that you need immediately, you can always download it manually from the *Help* menu by right-clicking on the black space beside *Now Playing*, selecting *Help* then selecting *Check for Updates...* (see Figure 10-2).

If you leave the *Download codecs automatically* checkbox selected, Media Player will try to source a codec for content it doesn't understand before telling you there was a problem.

If you don't want Media Player trying to go to the Internet if you try to play content of unknown format, uncheck this box. From a security perspective, you might prefer to maintain full control over what is and is not installed on your system.

Another convenient feature on this *Player Options* tab is the ability to make Media Player go into *Mini Player* mode when it starts playing content with a particular piece of metadata associated with it. In this way, you could use a playlist name (called *tunes for work* for example) and your desktop is automatically cleared for word processing or email.

Privacy settings (configured the first time you ran Media Player) can be revised through the *Privacy* tab, see Figure 10-3. You will see many of the settings you selected previously but you will also find that convenient shortcut to Internet Explorer for changing cookie privacy settings, and the ability to clear the Media Player history file and clear and cached content from your system.

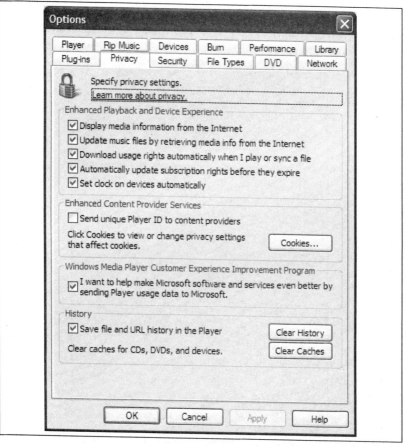

*Figure 10-3 Privacy settings can be
reconfigured if your preferences have changed
since initial setup*

Under the *Network* tab (see Figure 10-4) you can limit
the protocols and ports used by Media Player when

communicating over the network. You can also change the proxy settings for HTTP, MMS and RTSP used in case you are behind a proxy server.

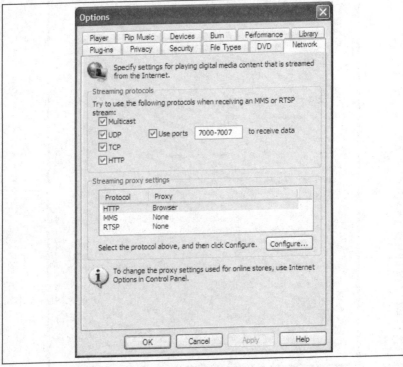

Figure 10-4 Use the Network settings to configure how Media Player works through a firewall

Finally, under the *Performance* tab, there are controls to adjust how Media Player communicates over your network connection (although the default setting where it detects the connection speed for you is by far the best), see Figure 10-5.

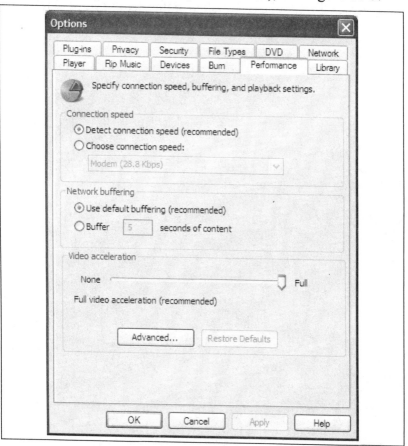

Figure 10-5 Change performance settings to suit your network connection speed and video hardware

You can adjust the amount of content buffered by Media Player before starting playback, although, again, you would need good motives to change this setting from default.

Appendix

The *PlaysForSure* logo shown in Figure A-1 is a compatibility rating awarded to media product vendors by Microsoft.

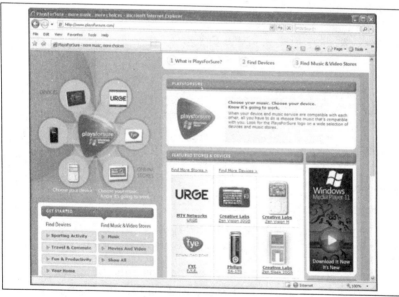

Figure A-1 PlaysForSure is the badge of Media Player compatibility

The website (http://www.playsforsure.com) is dedicated to the *PlaysForSure* experience where devices, software and vendors are showcased to have maximum exposure, see Figure A-1.

If you click on Find Devices (at the top of the homepage), you can browse through the device catalogue for something that suits your needs, see Figure A-2.

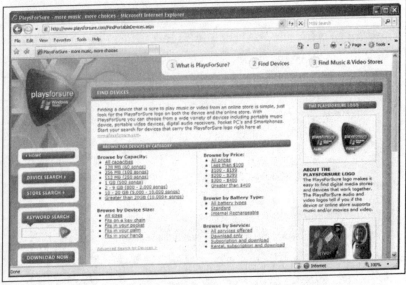

Figure A-2 Browse the catalogue for devices to suit your requirements

You will find that as the new world of online media starts to spread, more and more companies will jump on the bandwagon (no pun intended) and start producing their own online stores, new ways of acquiring content and a whole battalion of new portable devices will emerge in conjunction with the take-on of Microsoft Vista. Another example of one of the many new services available is Packard Bell's Music Station, seen here running inside Media Player in Figure A-3.

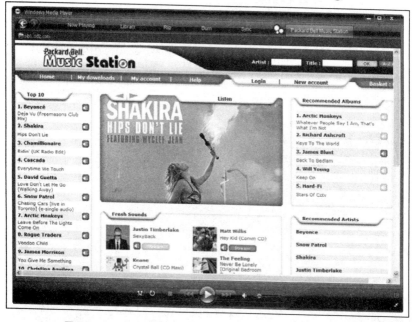

Figure A-3 Packard Bell's Music Station is yet another online media store vying for your business

A device and software combination that will certainly be compatible with Media Player 11 is Microsoft's attempt to compete in the currently Apple dominated *iTunes/iPod* marketplace. This device is called the *Zune*, and boasts a massive 30GB hard drive, wireless networking capability, 3-

inch high definition LCD screen that operates in both portrait and landscape mode (for widescreen presentations) as well as a built-in FM radio.

The device itself is a lightweight media player not unlike the *iPod,* and iPod fans will probably view it as a copycat product rather than anything truly innovative. In the picture of the *Zune* shown in Figure A-4, you can immediately see the similarities between it and the *iPod.*

Figure A-4 The Zune is stylish, well connected and versatile

The *Zune* software system will be completely compatible with both Media Player and *iTunes*, and you can choose to import all your songs from either of these two system into *Zune*, or leave your songs in Media Player. Songs left in *iTunes* will not be accessible to *Zune* users.

There are dozens more manufacturers specialising in digital media players that are compatible with Media Player 11. These are all listed on the *PlaysForSure* website.

There are many, many resources available for finding out more about Media Player and associated information. The rest of this Appendix introduces some of the best resources available on the Internet.

Microsoft

Microsoft (obviously) support the Media Player software itself but they also provide extensive resources for helping you to carry out your very own Media Player plug-in development and user interface customization, see Figure A-5.

*Figure A-5 Microsoft provides extensive
support for more than just Media Player 11*

To find out more about Media Player plug-ins and to try your
hand at some development yourself, try looking at the website,
http://www.microsoft.com/windows/windowsmedia/player/
plugins.aspx.

Creative Labs

Creative Labs have been in the portable media player business from the word go and have always been a front runner in the marketplace. Their devices are excellent and they provide a great support service for customers.

Figure A-6 Creative Labs have always been frontrunners in the development of outstanding media player products

Figure A-6 shows the Creative Labs homepage for portable media devices, listing a variety of their most modern products:

http://www.microsoft.com/windows/windowsmedia/player/plugins.aspx

Zune.net

As we've already discussed the *Zune* product, it's well worth popping along to the *Zune* website (http://www.zune.net) to check out what's on offer, see Figure A-7.

On the site you'll find resources on how to buy a *Zune* device, how to download and install the *Zune* software, how to determine compatibility requirements between your current system (for instance your *iPod/iTunes* setup) and the *Zune* system and how to access a plethora of online shopping resources that are compatible with *Zune* for shopping for content on the Internet.

*Figure A-7 Use Zune to merge your PC,
Internet and portable media systems into one
cohesive solution*

Archos

Archos are yet another purveyor of fine-quality portable media
systems and have plenty of products available that are
compatible with Media Player 11, see Figure A-8.

*Figure A-8 Archos are another of the front
runners in the portable media player
marketplace*

To find out more about Archos products and services,
visit their website at http://www.archos.com.

Sony

Last, but certainly not least, Sony (see Figure A-9) make a
wide variety of digital media products, some of which are

compatible with the Media Player 11 system. Make sure, however, you check for the *PlaysForSure* logo before you buy since Sony also produce a number of proprietary codec solutions that work a lot better with their own specialised software.

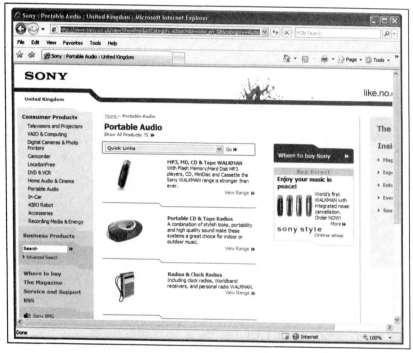

Figure A-9 Sony supply quality MP3 products as well as a variety of proprietary products that, although very good, are better suited to Sony software

For more information on Sony products in this category, go to their website at:

http://www.sony.co.uk/view/ShowProductCategory.action?site=odw_en_GB&category=Audio

Glossary

Broadband	A high-speed communications solution used for Internet access.
Burn	Term used to describe the creation of a CD or DVD, derived from the action of the laser on the surface of the disc.
Codec	A codec (from the linking of compressor/de-compressor) is a software module that turns digital music into playable formats for your PC.
Cookie	A cookie is used by websites to record information about you and your access to the site in order to make your web

	surfing experience a better and more seamless one.
HDTV	High definition television is the latest format for television broadcast with a much higher resolution than traditional television. HDTV is the format that all TV sets will understand and all broadcasting stations will broadcast in time.
Mini Player	The miniature Media Player 11 interface that attaches to the Vista taskbar. This facility is not available for Windows XP users.
MP3	The format most commonly used today for the encoding of digital music. Media Player 11 supports MP3 files by default.
PlaysForSure	The logo that signifies a device or website has been identified by Microsoft as compatible with Windows media solutions, such as

	Windows Media Player 11 and the Zune portable media device.
Playlist	A list of songs derived from your media library created from either a fixed set of selections or a dynamic rules-based selection. Playlists can be synchronized with portable media devices.
Plug-in	A plug-in is a piece of additional software that enables Media Player to connect to or process information not inherent in it by default. An example of a plug-in might be the MTV URGE software interface.
Privacy	This term relates to how you protect personal and private information of your own choosing, with privacy settings dictating which information can be readily shared with the public domain.

Rip	To rip a music track from a CD is to encode the audio format on a traditional CD into a PC readable format such as an MP3 file.
Shuffle	In Media Player terms, to shuffle is to randomly play music from the library – akin to party-mode on some devices.
URGE	MTV's online media store with millions of music tracks, music videos and radio channels to tune into.
Zune	A portable media device; Microsoft's answer to the *iPod*

Index

V

Z

Notes

Notes

Notes

Notes

Notes